# RIDING
## FOR THE
# KINGDOM

*The Cowboy Devotional*

Shakota Field

ISBN 978-1-68517-812-3 (paperback)
ISBN 978-1-68517-813-0 (digital)

Christian Faith Publishing
832 Park Avenue
Meadville, PA 16335
www.christianfaithpublishing.com

Cover Design Photo by Sarah Pfenninger

Printed in the United States of America

# Introduction

My name is Shakota Field. I would first like to say thank you for picking this book up and giving me a chance to give you a different way to think about things. I've been in the ranching industry my entire life, and I have also been a Christian and was raised in a Christian household. My brain has always had a unique way of making things make sense—or at least that is what I've been told.

I started writing a few things down and was encouraged to keep doing it by close friends. Then due to COVID, I lost my job and felt as if God called me to use my free time to write this devotional. It is aimed at giving cowboys a way to look at something we do day in and day out and apply it to our walk with the Lord. If you have never even touched a horse, I would still encourage you to give this book a try and see if it doesn't change the way you view some things.

There are only fourteen chapters, all of which are fairly short. I wouldn't call this book a teaching but more of a guide to help understand some of the complicated aspects of faith and how I dumbed them down for myself. Before reading each chapter, ask God to open your heart and help you to understand the message.

Thank you so much for picking this book up. It means the world to me. God bless you.

# Timing Is Everything

God's timing is perfect, right? Isaiah 60:22 tells us, "When the time is right I, the Lord will make it happen." That tells us that God's timing is perfect, but I know for me it doesn't always feel that way. The key here is that His timing is perfect for His plan, not ours.

When I think about timing, I always tend to think of a branding pen and flanking calves. Anyone that has flanked enough calves can tell you it's all about timing. If your timing is off, you're going to work your butt off and not get much done. When your timing is right, flanking is smooth and easy; but to have that timing, you must rely on the person on the rope.

Just in case you haven't spent much time in a branding pen, allow me to elaborate on that. Two guys flank and hold the calf down so we can vaccinate it. One on each side, one grabs the tail, and the other grabs the rope that is either on one or two back feet. The tail guy pulls, and then the rope guy, and the calf goes over on its side. I've seen real big strong guys get outflanked by sixteen-year-olds because they relied on timing and technique instead of muscle.

I don't know about anyone else, but I know I've showed up to a few places and thought, *Are we branding or weaning?* So I'd sneak around and find a good partner to flank with early. If my older brother was there, I would try my best to end up with him because we have flanked together for years and jive well together. It didn't matter if the calves weighed five hundred pounds. I was confident we could flank them without a problem. He is usually on the tail because it is easier for him to get up with all the metal in his back from a car wreck he had in 2012, and I prefer the rope, so it works out perfectly.

My job on the rope is to watch my brother and be patient. After he pulls, I pull, and nine out of ten times, the calf flops over. I don't watch the calf, really; aside from a little situational awareness, my eyes are on my brother. He determines when I pull by doing his job. If I focused on the calf instead of him, I would be late every time.

Let's take that same situation and look at it from a spiritual standpoint. God is on the tail; He pulls, but if I haven't prepared myself and I'm not in communication with Him and walking with Him, I may not be ready to do my part. It doesn't matter how much God pulls on the tail and sets the situation up for me to succeed if I'm not doing my part as well. If I have my eyes on the world and the situation instead of on God, I'm late.

I'm sure that if you've been around church very long, you have heard, "Don't worry, it just wasn't God's time for it to happen." Well, what if it was? What if God was doing His part, but we were so worried about the situation or what everyone would think or whatever excuse we use to avoid risk instead of watching God and pulling "the rope"?

One of my favorite things to do is to flank with younger/smaller kids. We've all been that little kid that can't wait until they are big enough to flank. Then one day, there is a smaller set of calves, and they get their chance. I enjoy that the most. I can get on the rope and control the situation (for the most part anyways) to make them successful. I have the power and the ability to flank those smaller calves by myself if I wanted to, but I always wait for them to pull. It doesn't matter if their technique is right or if they are a little timid or hesitant; I'm just waiting on the effort.

I wonder how many times we are on the tail of our purpose or the blessing God has for us or maybe in the answer to that prayer we say every night, and God is on the rope, watching us, waiting on us to pull. He's waiting for us to take that first step in faith. He has the power to do it by Himself but is going to help us succeed instead of handing it to us. You can be timid in that first step, but you can't be afraid to take it. I wonder how many blessings I've missed because I was afraid to pull.

The summed-up point of what I'm trying to say is simple. For God's timing to be perfect, we must be focused on Him and willing to "pull" when He sets up the situation for us. We serve a powerful God that can do anything He wants to at any time, but if we aren't serving Him or seeking out the purpose He has for our lives, we will miss the opportunity He has placed in front of us. So get in the Word, pray, and talk to our Father and don't be afraid to step out in faith and pull and watch what God will do in your life.

> And without the faith it is impossible to please God, because anyone who comes to him must believe that he exists and that he rewards those who earnestly seek Him. (Hebrews 11:6)

> He replied, "Because you have so little faith. Truly I tell you, if you have faith as small as a mustard seed, you can say to this mountain, 'Move from here to there,' and it will move. Nothing will be impossible for you." (Matthew 17:20)

# Cow Fight

As spring works are starting to kick off, I've been thinking a lot about big gathers and, more specifically, how they relate to our walk in faith. Just the other day, I was on a drive, and there was this one cow with the sole intention of running off and taking everything else with her. Any good cowboy knows he only has two options on how to handle her, and I want to talk about those and how we should handle this on a spiritual level.

So picture this: you are working with a dang good crew, the drive has just come together, and you can see the light at the end of the tunnel when that high-headed rip splits a gap and is gone. We leave her, right? It isn't the end of the world. We can always go catch her afterward, but she wouldn't be much fun in the pens anyways. But she left by herself, and that isn't good enough. So she hangs out and bawls or may even make a couple passes by the herd, trying to get some of her friends to come with her. Now you are stuck fighting the rest of the herd and get them penned, but the odds are you are going to lose a couple more, then some more, and the next thing you know, your horse is smoked, and you go home a loser.

Option two: once she cuts and runs, 'cause we all know she's going to, you rope her and tie her down. Right then, as soon as she tries, you bind her to something, be it a horse, a tree, or to herself with a string. Before she can even think about messing up the drive, she is caught and handled. The rest of the herd is penned without a problem, calves are worked, and it's a dang good day to be a cowboy.

That long-eared, high-headed cow is a problem we face every day, known as the devil. When we are called to do something for the kingdom of God, the devil will be out there in front, trying to derail you before you reach the pens. You can try to ignore it, and he will hit you little by little until you give up, whipped and pouting, headed back to the house. But if we bind him in the name of Jesus at the first sign, he becomes powerless.

The only difference between that aggravating cow and the devil is that the cow is easy to spot. The devil can come at you in many different ways. It could be a "friend" leading you away from your calling, could be your job and feeling like you're too busy for God to use you, or heck, it could be that broncy two-year-old that puts you into a bitter mood every day. All I'm trying to say is when that high-headed cow breaks and runs, don't be afraid to pull your rope down, and when the devil comes for your purpose, joy, family, or anything else for that matter, don't be afraid to call on Jesus because neither of them are worth your time or stress.

> I will give you the keys of the kingdom of heaven; whatever you bind on earth will be bound in heaven, and whatever you loose on earth will be loosed in heaven. (Matthew 16:19)

> When you become angry, don't let that anger make you sin. And don't continue to be angry all day. Don't give the devil a way to defeat you. (Ephesians 4:26–27)

# Pressure and Release

Growing up, I spent a lot of time on the fence of the round pen, watching my dad start colts. I learned a lot from watching him and my older brother, and then it was my turn to climb aboard and take my swing at being a horse trainer. One of the biggest parts of training young horses is pressure and release. I would put quite a bit of money on it that you could get the top ten trainers out there, and they would all agree that the release is crucial.

The easiest example that comes to mind is when you are asking a horse to back up and put pressure on their mouth with a bit and maybe even someone in front of them. The amount of pressure depends on the horse, but the release should always be the same. As soon as that horse starts backward, you release the pressure, rewarding them. Some horses pick this up a lot faster than others, and after a few rides, they understand giving in to the pressure means there will be a release. Others may take a little longer and a few more tricks. For example, I've seen many horses that get their heads tied down or around to one side or another until they learn to give in to that pressure.

Let's look at this from a spiritual standpoint for a minute. As Christians, we face a lot of different pressures, be it from the outside world or guilt from something we have done, and so on and so forth. We all handle pressure differently. Some of us feel a little pressure and are ready to give in, and for others, it takes a lot for us to break. But one thing is constant: God's release. The second we stop and step toward Him, there is release—release from guilt, release from habits, release from each and every sin we have done.

I'm going to tell you about a horse I bought when I was six or seven years old that was a hardheaded sucker. He hated grown men, but I could walk into any pasture, and he would walk up to me and be dog gentle. One day, my dad, my brother, and I were going to check some wheat pasture cattle, and my dad was going to ride that horse. Well, we got to the pasture. My brother and I unloaded our horses, but that horse refused to get out of the trailer.

Long story short, my brother and I checked that pasture; and when we got back to the trailer, that horse was still soled up, not wanting to get out. It didn't matter what we did. He was throwing a fit and wasn't going to cooperate. When we did finally get him out, that horse got to spend the rest of the day loading and backing out until he did it without hesitation. Had he got out the first time, the release of pressure would've been instant. But because he refused to give in and accept the pressure, the release didn't come.

At times, we can be like that horse. Instead of giving into God and accepting His release, we are stubborn and fight Him every step of the way. We stay in the same sin over and over instead of repenting which simply means to turn away from sin and toward God. Once we do that, we get the release which is God's grace and mercy.

I know that I have drawn this chapter out a bit. I could have said all this in the second paragraph, but this is by far the most important chapter in this book. Without this, none of the other chapters matter. I'm here to tell you it does not matter how stubborn you are, what you've done, or anything else. If you take that step to God and repent, you get the release—the release on all your past shortcomings and all the bad that makes you feel unworthy.

Jesus took the punishment for us, and all we have to do is accept Him into our heart. Romans 10:9 tells us, "If you declare with your mouth, 'Jesus is Lord,' and believe in your heart that God raised him from the dead, you will be saved." That is all it takes to get the greatest release in the world, and better yet, that will get your name written in the Lamb's Book of Life.

If we confess our sins, he is faithful and just and will forgive us our sins and purify us from all unrighteousness. (1 John 1:9)

For the Lord your God is gracious and compassionate. He will not turn his face from you if you return to Him. (2 Chronicles 30:9)

I tell you that in the same way there will be more rejoicing in heaven over one sinner who repents that over ninety-nine righteous persons who do not need to repent. (Luke 15:7).

# The Young Horse's First Drive

In the last chapter, we talked about starting young horses. We are going to stay on that same topic and go a little bit deeper into that process. It starts in the round pen; that's where you start building a relationship, so to speak, with the horse. Once you get that foundation started and some trust built up between each other, you take that next step and go outside. Doing this is a big step because you lose the safety and security that the round pen offers. Then the day comes that the young horse needs a job and is the one you catch to go to work.

Personally, I like to pick the day I take that horse. Either it's going to be a short day, I know the crew, and I won't be asked to do something I'm not mounted for; or I know the cows, and they are user-friendly. But sometimes it doesn't work out that way, and I end up asking that young horse to do a job that he isn't qualified for. Let's say we end up having a wreck, and calves need to be caught or possibly even a cow. Or the boss man asks me to watch a gate or help him sort some cows.

The jobs that could be asked of me go on and on, but you get the point. That horse is new to all this, and it's almost like I'm setting him up to fail. But I'm not asking the horse to know what to do. I'm simply asking him to stay between my hands and go where and when I tell him to. It may be his first time to see any of it, but I'm experienced enough to keep him safe and successful if he will follow me. With a good foundation and the colt being willing to do what I ask, we can do what was asked of us.

The church is our round pen. It's safe and secure, and we can start that relationship with God. Once our foundation is set comes the time to go outside. This may be reading your Bible daily or small groups that give you less security, but it's a big step in growing our relationship with God. Now it's time for a "job" or a better way to put it, time for our purpose to start. The purpose God has for life is different for everyone, but it usually starts with a calling.

That calling may be something you never thought possible or one that we don't feel qualified for or experienced enough to do right, and failure keeps us from trying. A great example of that is what you're reading right now. I was a B English student on a good year. Grammar and spelling are definitely not my strong suits, but the Lord told me to write, and I said, "Okay."

This is by far one of the scariest things I've done in life. Failure is always scary, but failing the Lord? That is terrifying. But I have a good foundation in Christ and a heart to please Him, so here I am, writing a book when I could barely write an essay in high school. The beauty is that when the Lord called me to this, He didn't ask for my report card or resume; He asked for my heart. I'm sure you've heard it before, but the Lord doesn't call those that are qualified. He qualifies the called.

God doesn't need us to know how to do what He has called us to do. He just needs us to listen to Him and go where and when He tells us. We may be inexperienced, and it may be the first time we are seeing it, but He can make us successful if we will just follow Him. The Bible shows us this again and again. I mean, was David qualified to kill Goliath?

I know that when I'm on that colt and the wreck happens, when that colt steps up and does the job I ask him, not because he knows to but because he trusts me enough to do it, I go home filled with joy and reward with some extra gain and a couple of days off.

I think the Lord does the same when He calls us to step out of the safety and security of our church, family, friend group, or whatever and go after what He has called us to do. When we do it, not because we know how, but we know He can do it through us, the amount of joy it must bring God to guide us and help us succeed in His purpose for our lives!

> Many are the plans in a person's heart, but it is the Lord's purpose that prevails. (Proverbs 19:20)

> The purposes of a person's heart are deep waters, but one who has insight draws them out. (Proverbs 20:5)

> And we know that in all things God works for the good of those who love him, who have been called according to his purpose. (Romans 8:28)

> "For I know the plans I have for you," declares the Lord, "plans to prosper you and not to harm you, plans to give you hope and a future." (Jeremiah 29:11)

# Drive Leader

During all the gathers that take place during spring and fall works, the most important job is that of the drive leader. His job is to lead everyone out and drop them off in their place to gather the pasture. The reason this is so important is that he may be the only one that knows the pasture or how to best go about making a successful gather. The success of how the gather goes depends on how it is dropped off.

As the drive leader, you have to know the country you are about to be gathering because more times than not, everyone else is following your lead. You either set them up for success or failure. For example, I was leading out a drive and decided to cut a corner because I hadn't seen cows there in weeks. When we got to the pens, we were short about a third of the herd.

Was that the fault of the guy I dropped off there? No, absolutely not. He followed my instructions and I lead him to failure at no fault of his own. My job as the drive leader is to not only lead by example, but also to be sure everyone is placed in a position they can handle. If I put the guy on the green broke colt in the hole that's the hardest to ride because the cows are going to try you the whole way, and something gets by him, that is also on me.

The placement of how you drop off the drive is so important. Let's say I have a crew of ten guys. Five have been in the pasture before, and five haven't. As the drive leader, I would stagger them. That way, if one of the guys new to the country starts to drift away from the spot he is riding, one of the guys beside him can bump him back onto the right path.

Although I can't always be there to guide them, I can still surround them with people that can. Now, I am well aware that every time you gather a pasture, it will always be different, but you can still send them prepared. I always like to point out a landmark that is close to the pens if I can. That way, if something happens, they can find their way back instead of ending up lost.

Now let's look at how this compares to our walk in faith. Guys, this one is pointed directly at you. As a man, you are called to be the leader of your household, especially after bringing children into the world. It is on your shoulders whether they end up at the gates of heaven or lost in the world when that final gather Jesus planned takes place. They are coming into the world blind, and it is our responsibility to guide them and to put them on a path to succeed not only in this life but in an eternal life. If we take shortcuts, they will follow in our footsteps and might fail at no fault of their own.

We have to lead by example and show our household how to live a godly life. For example, if every morning you got up and read your Bible at the table before breakfast, don't you think eventually your family would want to follow that instead of, let's say, watching the news and complaining about things out of your control?

The only way you can properly lead your household is if you know the path you are asking them to follow. This means being a godly man day in and day out, having a good relationship with our Creator, and giving your family a mold of what a person of God should look like.

Just like being a drive leader, it is important to surround your family with people that can bump them back onto the right path when they or even you start to drift. The Bible tells us, "As iron sharpens iron, so one person sharpens another" (Proverbs 27:17). The people you choose to allow around yourself and your household can either sharpen your spirit and push you to do better or hold you back from growing and achieving your purpose.

For example, when I was rodeoing growing up, I had free range at junior rodeos because my dad was the president of the association, and my mom was timing. But that didn't matter because I had many other "rodeo moms," and I can promise you if they saw me doing something bad, they would've whooped my butt. We can't always be there to watch over our family, but we can surround them with people who can. As godly people, we also need to be that for the people that allow us around their household. Don't be afraid to bump someone every now and then and correct their path.

My last point is probably the most important. Just like giving someone a landmark in a pasture, be sure your family has something to look for so when life gets a little crazy, they don't end up lost—whether that be a church, a small group, a Bible, or anything that can put them back on the path to the Father. We all reach for something, and I can tell you from experience that reaching for the Bible works a whole lot better than the bottle. It wouldn't be much fun to get to the pens just to find out your crew isn't coming.

> Train up a child in the way he should go;
> even when he is old he will not depart from it.
> (Proverbs 22:6)

> He must manage his own family well and see
> that his children obey him, and he must do so in
> a manner worthy of full respect. (1 Timothy 3:4)

# Night Latch

When it comes to riding colts or broncs or anything I don't really trust, I usually reach for my saddle that has a night latch on it. For those of you that don't know, a night latch is a strap around the swells of the saddle to hang on to if a horse was to start bucking. It is to keep you on the saddle instead of on the ground. The reason I use this saddle is because I know that no matter what that horse might try that day, I am prepared for it.

The only reason I am prepared for whatever that horse may do is because I have secured the night latch before he tries it. It has been permanently attached to the saddle and is regularly checked because when the time comes that I desperately need it, I won't have time to make sure it's ready.

For some of you reading this, it may not be that big of a deal; but to me, my night latch is a lifeline when a horse starts bucking. I cling to it until the bronc ride is over and then go on about my day. Without it, I would probably get bucked off and end up either hurt or walking.

Let's say I'm working somewhere, and other guys are counting on me to do my job, but I haven't prepared my night latch or I haven't looked at it in a while. Then the horse I'm on decides to buck, I reach for my lifeline, but it's either not there or has been neglected for so long that it breaks. Now I'm in the dirt, and now the job I was supposed to do is left unfinished because I didn't prepare myself for the bronc ride.

Not only did I let the people around me down, but they will probably end up looking for me and not get their job done either. This whole situation could have easily been avoided had I just taken five minutes out of my day to check on my gear and be sure I was prepared for when the fight happened.

God provides all of us with a night latch to cling to when life tries to buck us off. But for many of us, we haven't taken the time to attach it to our everyday life. The Bible is a great lifeline for us. So many of the struggles we face are laid out in front of us—if we would just take the time to read it and apply God's Word to that situation!

However, this is only possible if we are preparing ourselves before the fight happens. More times than not, we don't have time to go get our Bibles or even google scriptures when life gets crazy. But if we would take five minutes a day and get in the Word, when trouble comes, it's already in our heart to cling on to.

When we aren't prepared for those fights, we become easy targets for the devil to discourage. Instead of clinging to the Word and making it through the fight and fulfilling our purpose, we end up not only in the dirt but maybe even walking down a different path. The Word of God is such a powerful tool that God gave us to help us every day. But much like a night latch, some of us feel as if we either don't need it or don't think we can understand it—or at least I know that was my excuse until I did it.

The struggle in life is a given. There is always going to be something happening to knock us down. But if we would cling to our Bible the same way I cling to a night latch when a horse blows up, I know it would be easier to take those things in stride knowing that what He is doing through us is beyond worth the struggle we are facing.

> For everything that was written in the past was written to teach us, so that through the endurance taught in the Scriptures and the encouragement they provide we might have hope. (Romans 15:4)

Every word of God proves true; he is a shield to those who take refuge in Him. (Proverbs 30:5)

Put on the full armor of God, so that you can take stand against the devil's schemes. (Ephesians 6:11).

# Watching the Gate

We've talked a lot about the drive and getting to the pens, but what happens after you make the drive is just as important. Once you are in the security of the pens, the work is long from over. Now it is time to strip the calves, or separate them from their mothers so we can work them. This can be a very simple fast task or a long drawn-out one, depending on who is watching the gate.

Getting asked to watch the gate is an honor because it means the boss either thinks a lot of you and your ability or thinks a lot of your horse. It is also a lot of responsibility. Everyone else will bring you a drag of cattle, and it's on you to let the cows by and cut the calves back.

When this is done right, it's a cool thing to watch. Everything works smoothly. Once you finish, you can get straight to branding, and it makes for a good day. Missing one or two isn't the end of the world or anything to hang your head about either. Everyone falls short, and that mistake can be corrected pretty easily with a rope. Two guys can ride and rope the calves, and you're back on track.

On the other hand, if the guy on the green broke colt that takes an acre to turn is in the gate and half the herd of calves get by, that is a different story. Now it has turned into another job to do instead of a simple fix. Every calf that you allow through that gate is a different problem. One or two is fine, but twenty or thirty, and you might as well just start all over. Don't get me wrong. It can always be fixed, but it would have been much simpler had we just stopped them at the gate.

Now let's add a little extra pressure. This spring, we gathered a pasture into a set of portable pens. When we stripped that gate led back into the pasture meaning it was very important that nothing got by that wasn't meant to. We had a few guys sitting outside the gate with ropes down as a safety net, but cutting them at the gate before they were able to run wild is the best way to avoid a wreck. The guy on the best horse got in the gate, and we stayed slow and easy trying to funnel only cows to the gate. When a calf got by us in the pen, the gate man turned it back, shutting the problem down before it became one.

From the spiritual side of things, salvation is the most important, but just because you are saved doesn't mean the work is done. Just like once you get to the pens during a cow drive, now it's time to separate the worldly things from the godly things in life. This is a lot easier said than done. However, the best way to do it is to stop it at the gate. That may not make sense, but just hang with me for a minute. Every action or word that comes out of our mouths all starts as a thought.

By policing our thoughts constantly and deciding then if it is to honor God or not is the best way to live a godly lifestyle. For me, it has come naturally to have a heart for the Lord, but a brain for the Lord? That is a different story. But once I started sitting in the gate of my thoughts and started turning the worldly ones back instead of having to deal with the repercussions once they got past the gate and turned into actions, it has gotten easier. Just like the calves, each worldly action is a problem in itself. Some can be caught easily, and others grow and develop into a habit that becomes hard to kick.

The good news is that they can all be fixed. There is not a problem in this world too big for God.

He is our safety net, so to speak, because we all fall short of His glory daily, but Jesus took our punishment to deliver us from those actions. But just because we have a safety net behind us doesn't mean we should allow everything through the gate. Just like in that set of portable pens, it may be necessary to go slow and filter certain things extra. For example, you may need to filter what you look at on a day-to-day basis or what you drink or even who you are around. Once you do this, the easier it gets to live a godly life.

He will be a spirit of justice to the ones who sits in judgment, and a source of strength to those who turn back the battle at the gate. (Isaiah 28:6)

Make a tree good and its fruit will be good, or make a tree bad and its fruit will be bad, for a tree is recognized by its fruit. (Matthew 12:33)

Above all else, guard your heart, for everything you do flows from it. Keep your mouth free of perversity; keep corrupt talk far from your lips. Let your eyes look straight ahead; fix your gaze directly before you. Give careful thought to the paths for your feet and be steadfast in your ways. Do not turn to the right or the left; keep your foot from evil. (Proverbs 4:23–27)

# Grubbing

Today, I was sitting on an excavator grubbing a pasture because it had been overrun with mesquite trees. Mesquite trees are an invasive species that were never supposed to be in that pasture. They disrupt the natural course of the pasture by taking away water and sunlight from the grass. We could go in with a bulldozer or spray the trees to knock them down for a little while, but they will continue to grow back. The only way to truly rid the pasture of the mesquite is to dig up the root.

This job can be tedious and boring. It sure isn't something I jump out of bed excited to go do, but if it goes undone, before long, the pasture will be all mesquite with no grass and can no longer serve its purpose. Depending on how long the trees have been there, digging up the roots can be easier said than done. The little ones are pretty easy, but a tree that has been there for years has developed deep hard roots that are difficult to pull up. They tend to break, leaving behind enough for it to grow back, so you have to really take your time and be sure you get it all.

There are also times you run into multiple trees feeding off the same root system. This makes it difficult to find the main stem to dig up. But after doing so, the pasture can better serve its purpose and produce what it was originally intended to. Keep in mind that grubbing does not leave the pasture in its original condition. Digging up roots leaves behind holes and dead trees that have to be cleaned up, but over time and proper care, the pasture can return to grass, and you would never know the damage the mesquite caused.

As Christians, we go through the same thing as that pasture. Something that God never intended for us enters our lives. Whether it comes from a bad decision or something we had no control over, it plants a seed that grows into something taking us away from our purpose. This could be a couple of different things, such as bitterness, fear, anxiety, or depression. Or it could be a coping mechanism that turns into an addiction or a sinful mindset.

As humans, a lot of times, we try to hide that problem, much like knocking down the trees, but no matter how deep you think you have buried it, the root is intact and will find its way to the surface. Once it does that, it can spread to other areas, further hindering you from the purpose God has for your life.

The only way to truly heal the damaged areas is to expose the root of it and give it to God. Just like the mesquite tree, this can be easier said than done. The hurt that has been buried for years is not fun to dig up and leaves behind holes. However, if we don't do this, it will continue to affect our lives negatively. After we dig up these roots, it opens up a new part of our lives that God can use to help us prosper. God can take the deepest, darkest, damaged part of you and grow it into something serving His glory if we allow Him to.

> Therefore, if anyone is in Christ, he is a new creation. The old has passed away; behold the new has come. (2 Corinthians 5:17)

> If we confess our sins, he is faithful and just to forgive us our sins and to cleanse us from all unrighteousness. (1 John 1:9)

> Behold, I will bring to it health and healing, and I will heal them and reveal to them abundance of prosperity and security. (Jeremiah 33:6)

# Mass Treating

From the time I was three until I was through college, my dad was the cattle manager at a seven-thousand-head feedlot, which meant when I wasn't in school, I was at work with him. Being with him day in and day out during summer vacation taught me a lot about the management of cattle. We pulled and treated sick cattle, shipped and received, and processed and sorted the fats to ship to the packing house. I'd like to think that I'm pretty well-rounded, but the thing that always seemed most important to me was mass treating.

We would get a lot of high-risk sale barn cattle in during the month of July, so it was always a decision on whether to mass treat them or not. The vets that I've talked to have all said once you have a 10 percent pull rate on that set of cattle, it is better to go ahead and mass treat everything. So in a sense, 10 percent can bless the herd. Once the decision is made to mass treat, every animal is run through a chute and given an antibiotic shot. Doing this can be expensive and can make it more difficult to make a profit if the cattle don't perform well. So it takes a little faith that putting the money down up-front will keep the cattle heathier, which makes them eat, putting on weight faster, which means less days on feed.

But what if you are on a tight budget? Let's say that shot seems a little too expensive, and you can't justify spending that money on something that isn't a guarantee. Roll the dice and just keep pulling and treating. The next thing you know, you have a 10 percent death loss, and when it comes time to ship, you lose money on that set of cattle. Now you're wishing you had mass treated them, knowing the outcome is bad, but that's the thing about it—if you don't do it in the beginning, you can't do it at all.

I'm sure you already know where I'm going with this, but let's look at this from a spiritual standpoint. Tithing is one of the most important things when it comes to our walk with God, in my opinion. Not only is it showing faith in God to take care of us, but it allows Him to bless us. There is a catch, though. The tithe must come first. It can't come after all the bills are paid and there is still enough left over.

God has to come first in all things, especially money. Matthew 6:24 tells us, "No one can serve two masters, for either he will hate the one and love the other, or he will be devoted to the one and despise the other. You cannot serve God and money."

I know that sometimes this is easier said than done. Some months, money is tight, and the heater has to stay on, but that is when I think tithing is most important. When we have the faith to tithe even though it looks like we may come up short, God will honor that and you. "I am the vine; you are the branches. If you remain in me and I in you, you will bear much fruit; apart from me you can do nothing" (John 15:5).

When we tithe, we are allowing God into our finances, which allows Him to bless our finances. Just like mass treating cattle, if 10 percent can bless the herd and be more profitable, why not let it?

What if I told you that tithing is so important that even God did it? John 3:16 is a verse that most people know. It says, "For God so loved the world he gave his one and only Son, that whoever believes in him shall not perish but have eternal life." God gave His only Son first in hopes that we would believe in Him. There was no guarantee, but out of faith and love, He gave to us.

If you want to get more in-depth about what tithing really is, look up Transformation Church on YouTube. They have a six-part series that is very eye-opening. But I would like to challenge you to mass treat your money. Give God 10 percent and watch what He can do in your life. I'm not telling you by doing so you'll get rich, but when we do this, we open up and allow God to bless our lives, not just our wallets.

"Bring the full tithe into the storehouse, that there may be food in my house. Test me in this," says the Lord, "and see if I will not throw open the floodgates of heaven and pour out so much blessing that there will not be room enough to store it." (Malachi 3:10)

One gives freely, yet grows all the richer; another withholds what he should give, and only suffers want. (Proverbs 11:24)

Give and it will be given to you. Good measure, pressed down, shaken together, running over, will be put into your lap. For the measure you use it will be measured back to you. (Luke 6:38)

# Gather Your Country

When the drive leader drops you off, that means he just assigned you "your country," which is either between the guy on either side of you or the fence and the person next to you. The cattle in that part of the pasture are now your responsibility to gather above anything else.

Let's say you are gathering and see something happening two guys over and decide to ride over there to help or even tell them what they need to do, and while you're there, you miss something in your country. Now the drive leader is going to be on your butt for not doing your job. There is no excuse because the wreck happened where you were supposed to be. The only exception is if you bump over to the guy next to you to get him back on track, then go back to your spot.

I learned this the hard way when I was about seventeen. I thought pretty highly of myself, and the guy next to me wasn't doing a very good job, so I decided I would go do it for him. While I was worried about his job, I didn't go to a corner and missed about forty cows that were standing in it.

When we got to the pens, I was the one getting yelled at because while I was doing his job, I failed to do my own. Had I gone over and helped him then returned to my spot, all would have been good. If he didn't make it to the pens, that would have been on him because it was his job. But me being a hotshot kid trying to outdo him and prove I was better got my butt chewed and embarrassed for not getting my cows to the pens.

This same thing can be applied to our daily lives. We all have our own life to live. Sure, we can try our best to lead by example and help others get on the right path, but at the end of the day, that is up to them. We have to focus on our lives and living a godly life, and when the times comes, be sure the gates of heaven open and welcome us. It is much easier to look down and judge those doing wrong, but if we focus on that, we might end up missing our calling or a way to help them.

When that day comes, we won't have to answer to any of their sins, just our own. Every day, we should focus on being the best we can and try to lead people to God's glory instead of the wrong they are doing. Matthew 7:3–4 tells us, "Why do you look at the speck of sawdust in your brother's eye and pay no attention to the plank in your own eye? How can you say to your brother, 'Let me take the speck out of your eye,' when all the time there is a plank in your own eye?" This very simply tells us to focus on our own faults instead of the faults of others, even though seeing others is much easier.

> There is only one lawgiver and judge, he
> who is able to save and destroy. But who are you
> to judge your neighbor? (James 4:12)

# Coming Up Short

When gathering cattle, coming up short is going to happen from time to time. This could be caused by someone not paying attention, being shorthanded, or maybe the county is just rough and the cows outsmart you. Depending on the situation, this could be an easy fix of just leaving the ones you missed or you may be heading back to find them.

I remember a time that eight of us gathered this rough bushy pasture that was half miserable to get around in. When we got to the pens, we were one cow short. One of the guys said he saw one run off, but he wasn't close enough to even attempt to get around her, so we sat there and discussed our options, and the boss man informed us we had to go back and find her. I was annoyed when he said that because not only did we have to make an entire drive to find her, but my horse was tired, and it was getting plenty hot.

We struck out and rode and rode, looking in every nook and cranny, not finding any sign of this cow, but we kept after it. The day dragged on, everyone getting a little more annoyed the hotter it got. Then the guy to my left finally hollered he had his eyes on her. We all came running to be sure that she didn't slip away again and got her to the pens and loaded on the trailer. All of that took us an additional four hours and the majority of the afternoon, which seemed like a waste of time to me, but to the owner, it was necessary. He was hauling those cows to the sale, and every dollar counted, so to him, leaving her wasn't an option.

As Christians, every one of us comes up short in one way or another every single day. Luckily for us, Jesus doesn't hesitate to saddle up and come back for us. Matthew 18:12 tells us this: "What do you think? If a man owns a hundred sheep, and one of the them wanders away, will he not leave the ninety-nine on the hills and go back to look for the one that wandered off?" That tells me that it does not matter how far we venture off down our own path. Jesus is going to be right there to guide us back. The following verse goes on to say, "And if he finds it, truly I tell you, he is happier about that one sheep than about the ninety-nine that did not wander off."

Jesus made the gather on the cross so that all that accept Him in their hearts can have eternal life in heaven, but I'm here to tell you that He would make that same sacrifice again just for you to have that same eternal life, if that's what it would take. If you haven't ever made that step and you're still hiding in the brush and would like to step out, Romans 10:9 tells us all you have to do is, "If you declare with your mouth 'Jesus is Lord' and believe in your heart that God raised him from the dead, you will be saved." That simple prayer will have all of heaven rejoicing because you have now walked into the pens.

> For everyone that calls on the name of the Lord will be saved. (Romans 10:13)

> It is the Lord who goes before you. He will be with you; he will not leave you nor forsake you. Do not fear or be dismayed. (Deuteronomy 31:8)

# Riding for the Brand

If you are involved in any sort of cowboying role or have been around it very much, then I'm sure you've heard the term "ride for the brand." If you haven't, it's a pretty simple concept. It basically means that you represent that ranch, and you treat it as if it is your own. Just like any company expects when you go to a public place with something tying you to that ranch (a brand, a shirt, a vehicle, etc.), you are supposed to act in a way that reflects good on the ranch.

A great example of this is the WRCA finals in November. There are teams from all over that come to showcase their skills, all of which are connected to a ranch. Believe it or not, seeing you and how you act during those four days may be how some people perceive that ranch for the rest of their lives. In fact, to some people that have never been around cowboys, that might be how they look at the whole ranching industry for the rest of their lives.

This means if you are throwing a fit after a bad run or at the bar, stumbling drunk, starting fights, they might think every cowboy is a drunk idiot that throws fits. On the other hand, if you keep your composure and use the manners your momma taught you, they might wish the world had more cowboys, or might inspire some kids to look up to you and join the industry we all love. For a lot of the people in town, you are the closest they will ever get to a ranch, so they carry the impression you give them across to all of us.

The same thing can be said about being a Christian. For so many people, the closest they may get to a church or opening a Bible may be talking to you or even watching you, for that matter. If they can see God's light shining through you in the way you handle yourself and speak, they might want to get some of that for themselves. But if instead of opening a lost soul with open arms, we look down on the things they do, we may be the reason they never give God a second chance.

We should carry ourselves in a way that when people see us, they think, *I want what they have.* I know that is a lot easier said than done, but I've heard too many people say they "didn't feel welcome in church or by Christians." We should ride for the kingdom of God and try to encourage as many people as we can to join us there.

> But in your hearts honor Christ the Lord as holy, always being prepared to make a defense to anyone who asks you for a reason for the hope that is in you; yet do it gentleness and respect. (1 Peter 3:15)

> Nor do people light a lamp and put it under a basket, but on a stand, and it gives light to all in the house. In the same way, let your light shine before others, so that they may see your good works and give glory to your Father who is in heaven. (Matthew 5:15–16)

# Shipping Day

For the last four years, I managed a ranch in the panhandle of Texas. For the most part, all the decisions were made by me as far as herd health and when works would take place as far as branding and shipping. My boss didn't come see me or check up on me until it was shipping day, then we would drive around and evaluate the job I had done over the last year. If he liked what he saw, I got a pat on the back and kept my job; if not, it could have been my last day.

My job hinged on that one day, but it took me all year to prepare for that one day. It took constant work to better the ranch, feed the cows, make sure the calves stayed healthy and would be ready when it came time to ship. Had I decided to wait until the day my boss showed up to try to get ready, he would have been disappointed with what he found. I had to stay ready and be sure the rest of the ranch was ready day in and day out because once I saw the semis and his pickup pull through the gate, it was too late.

Whether we are in the end-times or not, I can't say for sure, but what I am positive of is that Jesus is coming back. Matthew 24:36 tells us, "Concerning that day and hour no one knows, not even the angels of heaven, nor the Son, but the Father only." This tells me that we should be preparing every single day for His return because once we hear the trumpets, it is much too late. Just like it was for me on the ranch, to be prepared when that day comes, it takes constant work, making sure we are walking in faith and know in our hearts that Jesus in Lord.

The fact that He is coming back should also push us to encourage all of our friends and families to be prepared at any given moment as well. Matthew 24:44 says this perfectly: "Therefore you also must be ready, for the Son of Man is coming at an hour you do not expect." I know when the clouds open, and I see Jesus's face coming to earth, I want to have no doubt that I did my part to bring all my brothers and sisters home. We can't sit around and wait on the right time because He is coming back like a thief in the night, and we can't be caught off guard.

> But know this, that if the master of the house had known at what hour the thief was coming, he would not have left his house to be broken into. (Luke 12:39)

# Waiting on the Squall

When making big drives gathering big country, the majority of the time, the drive leader will drop you off and say something along the lines of, "I'll holler when I hit the corner." Depending on where you are in the drive, this could take five minutes or up to forty-five minutes.

This can be hard to sit and wait on. You start feeling like maybe you missed it and now you're behind the drive. Sitting there in the silence, no one in sight, ten minutes feels like an hour. There have even been mornings that I hear a cow bawl, and I want to strike out on my own because I'm tired of waiting. I'm tired of being still and I feel like I need to see what the people around me are doing.

If I were to strike out on my own, I would end up on my own path instead of what the boss man has planned for me and could very well end up turning the cows back on the guys next to me. Or I could end up in front of cows that are kicked to me by my next man and totally miss the reason I was put in the position to begin with.

This is a pretty common thing to struggle with as a Christian, especially in the cowboy world. It is hard for us to sit still and wait for God to send us. Instead, we want to do it for ourselves. Sitting in silence, waiting for the answer to your prayers, time tends to drag on. Or our mind can play tricks on us, and we think we are being sent, when in reality, it's just the world telling us we are behind.

Maybe you're waiting on a relationship, a home, a job, or even a child, and your prayer feels like it's falling on deaf ears. If we decide to jump on the opportunity that walks by instead of the one that

God is sending us on, we can end up off course and against the will He has for our lives. We may not be in the right spot when the blessing He has for us presents itself.

This is one of those things that is dang sure easier said than done. I know I struggle with it daily, but I truly believe if we would pray in the silence instead of worry, God will bless us beyond our wildest dreams.

> I consider that our present sufferings are not worth comparing with the glory that will be revealed in us. (Romans 8:18 NIV)

> I am going to send you what my Father has promised; but stay in the city until you have been clothed with power from on high. (Luke 24:49)

> Wait for the Lord; be strong and take heart and wait for the Lord. (Psalm 27:14 NIV)

# About the Author

My name is Shakota Field. I've always been very passionate about two things: God and cowboying. This book gave me the chance to combine my passions.

CPSIA information can be obtained
at www.ICGtesting.com
Printed in the USA
BVHW031351110422
633959BV00006B/206